TYRANNOSAURUS

by Janet Riehecky
illustrated by Diana Magnuson

THE CHILD'S WORLD

MANKATO, MN

*Grateful appreciation is expressed to Bret S. Beall,
Curatorial Coordinator for the Department of Geology,
Field Museum of Natural History, Chicago, Illinois,
who reviewed this book to insure its accuracy.*

Library of Congress Cataloging in Publication Data

Riehecky, Janet, 1953-
  Tyrannosaurus / by Janet Riehecky ; illustrated by Diana L.
Magnuson.
    p. cm. — (Dinosaurs)
    Summary: Discusses what is known and what is hypothesized about
the dinosaur that terrorized other dinosaurs.
    ISBN 0-89565-424-5
    1. Tyrannosaurus—Juvenile literature. [1. Tyrannosaurus
rex.] I. Magnuson, Diana, ill. II. Title. III. Series: Riehecky,
Janet, 1953-   Dinosaurs.
QE862.S3R54   1988
567.9'7—dc19   88-1692
                                                   CIP
                                                    AC

      5 6 7 8 9 10 11 12 R 97 96 95 94 93 92

TYRANNOSAURUS

Before people lived on the earth, dinosaurs roamed the world.

It was a dangerous world then. But dinosaurs had many ways to protect themselves.

Some were small and fleet-footed. When
trouble came, they just ran away.

Some were too big to be able to move
quickly. When trouble came near them,
they just moved together and formed a
wall.

Others were protected by armor on their bodies. Animals that tried to bite an armored body might end up breaking their teeth.

Still others used parts of their bodies as weapons. They used the horns on their heads or clubs on their tails against enemies.

But there was one kind of dinosaur that didn't care what the other dinosaurs did to protect themselves—it would get them anyway! That dinosaur was the Tyrannosaurus!

The Tyrannosaurus (ti-ran-o-SAWR-us), whose name means "tyrant lizard," was the biggest meat eater ever to live on the earth. There were dinosaurs that grew bigger than the Tyrannosaurus, but they were gentle plant eaters. There was nothing gentle about Tyrannosaurus!

The Tyrannosaurus could grow twenty feet tall (that's more than three times as tall as your father), fifty feet long (that's longer than a city bus), and weighed more than seven tons (that's 14,000 pounds!). And every bit of the Tyrannosaurus was designed for hunting.

thick, muscular tail

huge, muscular legs

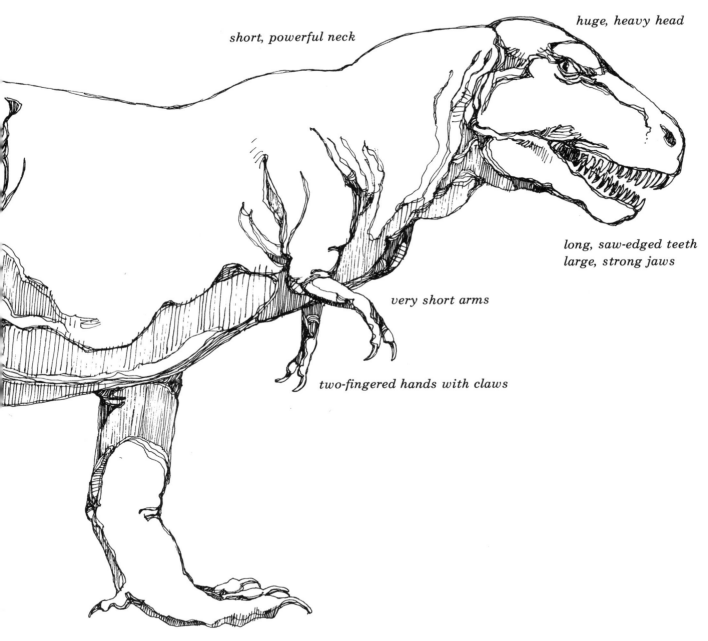

short, powerful neck

huge, heavy head

long, saw-edged teeth
large, strong jaws

very short arms

two-fingered hands with claws

four toes with long, sharp claws;
one toe turned back

The Tyrannosaurus walked on its two
back legs, towering over the countryside.
Those legs were very strong. Some scientists think they were strong enough to let
the Tyrannosaurus chase its prey at
speeds as fast as 30 miles per hour—

at least for a short distance. And then
when Tyrannosaurus caught its prey, the
three sharp claws on each foot became
fearsome weapons!

Even more frightening, though, were the teeth of the Tyrannosaurus. They were more than six inches long with very sharp edges. Some scientists think the Tyrannosaurus killed its prey by just running at it with its mouth open and those awful teeth sticking out. This would save time. When the two would collide, the Tyrannosaurus would already have its first mouthful!

The Tyrannosaurus' big head also contained a fairly big brain—bigger than a human brain. But that didn't mean that the Tyrannosaurus was as smart as a person. Only a small part of that brain was for thinking (probably about its next meal). Most of the brain controlled how the Tyrannosaurus could see and smell (the better to track down its next meal!).

It would seem that a dinosaur like the Tyrannosaurus couldn't have a problem at all. But it did—a very strange problem. Scientists think that if the Tyrannosaurus lay down, it had trouble getting back up. And this was a dinosaur who couldn't wait to get up in the morning—for breakfast!

The Tyrannosaurus' arms were much too small and weak to push itself up. In fact, scientists wondered for years why the Tyrannosaurus even had those little-bitty arms—they weren't even long enough to reach the Tyrannosaurus' mouth.

Then one scientist suggested what
those arms might have been used for.
Each hand had two fingers with long
claws. If the Tyrannosaurus dug those
claws into the ground, they would keep it
from slipping. Then it could use its strong
back legs to lift its body.

We don't know if this is true or not, but
it might be that those tiny arms were all
that kept the mighty Tyrannosaurus
from falling on its nose.

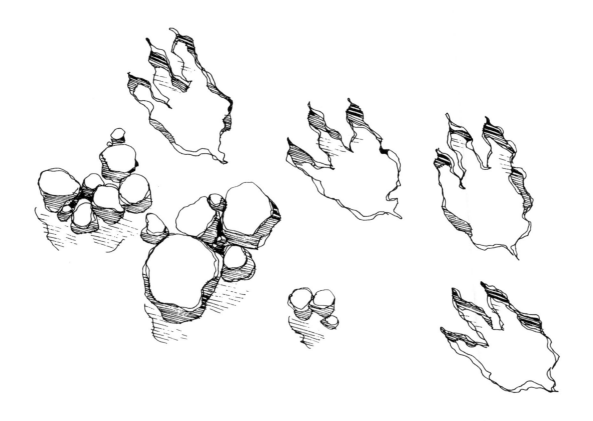

Not much is known about the family life of the Tyrannosaurus. The tracks that have been found suggest that most Tyrannosaurs traveled alone or in pairs. Apparently, they didn't like each other any more than the other dinosaurs liked them.

They probably laid eggs, but scientists
don't know if the mothers took care of the
babies when they hatched or just left the
babies to take care of themselves.

Scientists continue to study the Tyrannosaurus, hoping to find the answers to
these and other questions.

The Tyrannosaurus was one of the last of the dinosaurs to die, but it died out just as all the other dinosaurs did 65 million years ago.

Scientists don't know whether a sudden catastrophe killed all the dinosaurs, or whether they just gradually died off.

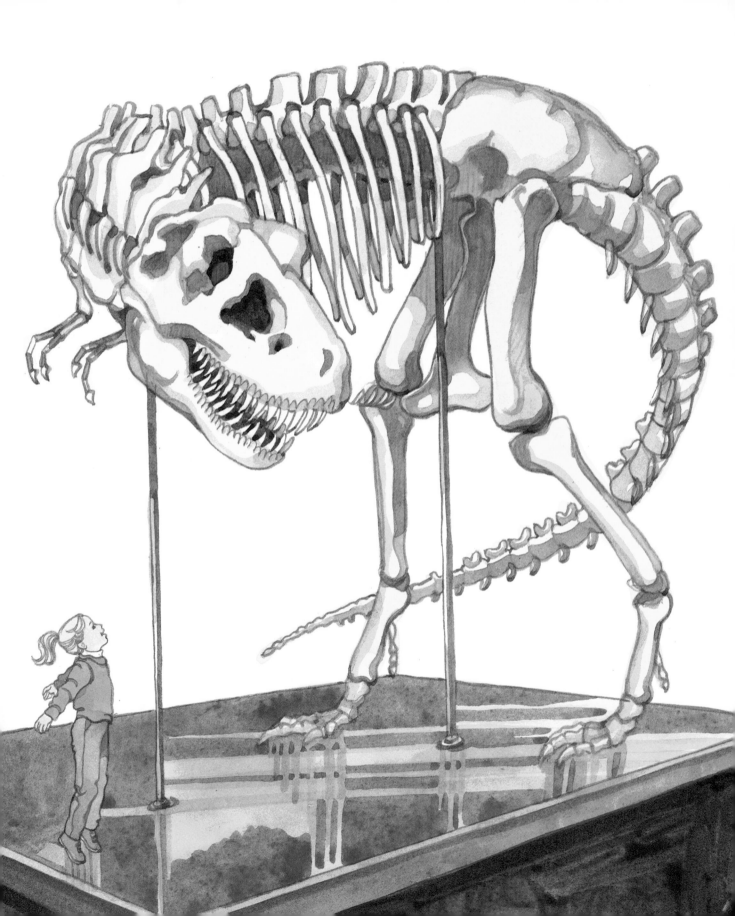

It could be that a terrible disease spread through the world. Or that the food supply disappeared. Or that the earth became too hot or too cold for dinosaurs to live. We may never know for sure.